# Rookie National Parks™

# Hawai'i Volcanoes National Park

## by Karina Hamalainen

### Content Consultant

Nanci R. Vargus, Ed.D.
Professor Emeritus, University of Indianapolis

### Reading Consultant

Jeanne M. Clidas, Ph.D.
Reading Specialist

**Children's Press®**
An Imprint of Scholastic Inc.

Library of Congress Cataloging-in-Publication Data
Names: Hamalainen, Karina, author.
Title: Hawai'i Volcanoes National Park/by Karina Hamalainen.
Description: New York: Children's Press, an imprint of Scholastic Inc.,
[2019] | Series: Rookie national parks | Includes index.
Identifiers: LCCN 2018023403| ISBN 9780531133200 (library binding) |
ISBN 9780531137239 (pbk.)
Subjects: LCSH: Hawaii Volcanoes National Park (Hawaii)—Juvenile literature.
| Volcanoes—Hawaii—Juvenile literature.
Classification: LCC DU628.H33 H356 2019 | DDC 551.2109969/1—dc23

Produced by Spooky Cheetah Press
Design: Ed LoPresti Graphic Design
Creative Direction: Judith E. Christ for Scholastic Inc.

Published in 2019 by Children's Press, an imprint of Scholastic Inc.

Printed in North Mankato, MN, USA 113

SCHOLASTIC, CHILDREN'S PRESS, ROOKIE NATIONAL PARKS™, and
associated logos are trademarks and/or registered trademarks of Scholastic Inc.

1 2 3 4 5 6 7 8 9 10 R 28 27 26 25 24 23 22 21 20 19

Scholastic, Inc., 557 Broadway, New York, NY 10012.

Photos ©: cover: Danita Delimont/Getty Images; back cover: Doug Perrine/NPL/Minden
Pictures; "Ranger Red Fox" by Bill Mayer for Scholastic; 1-2: Cleo Design/Shutterstock; 3:
USGS; 4-5: Jim Sugar/Getty Images; 6-7: Douglas Peebles/Getty Images; 8: Douglas Peebles/
Robert Harding Picture Library; 9: Chris Stewart/AP Images; 10-11: Mint Images/Aurora
Photos; 12-13 background: Olivera White/Alamy Images; 13 inset: Corbis/Getty Images;
14-15: Doug Perrine/NPL/Minden Pictures; 16 inset: National Park Service; 16-17 background:
Daniel Kirchner/iStockphoto; 18-19: National Park Service; 20: fisheyeimaging/age fotostock;
21: Jack Jeffrey/Photo Resource Hawaii; 22 left: Leighton Lum/Photo Resource Hawaii; 22 right:
Stock Connection/Superstock, Inc.; 23: Maremagnum/Getty Images; 24-25 background:
G. Brad Lewis/Photo Resource Hawaii; 24 inset: G. Brad Lewis/Photo Resource Hawaii; 26
top left: Martin Harvey/Getty Images; 26 top center: Jared Hobbs/Getty Images; 26 top
right: RugliG/Shutterstock; 26 bottom left: Greg Vaughn/Getty Images; 26 bottom center: Mc
Cormick, Victoria/Animals Animals; 26 bottom right: Masa Ushioda/age fotostock/Superstock,
Inc.; 27 top left: Joel Sartore, National Geographic Photo Ark/Getty Images;
27 top right: George Rose/Getty Images; 27 bottom left: Frederic Desmette/Biosphoto/Minden
Pictures; 27 bottom center: Doug Perrine/NPL/Minden Pictures; 27 bottom right: Dominique
Delfino/Getty Images; 30 top left: senlektomyum/Shutterstock; 30 top right: FlaviaMarie/
Shutterstock; 30 bottom left: Eyewave/Dreamstime; 30 bottom right: LAURA_VN/Shutterstock;
31 top: G. Brad Lewis/Aurora Photos; 31 center top: David Reggie/Getty Images; 31 bottom:
Luis Castaneda Inc./Getty Images; 31 center bottom: Olivera White/Alamy Images; 32: Inigo
Cia/Getty Images

Maps by Jim McMahon/Mapman®

# Table of Contents

I am Ranger Red Fox, your tour guide. Are you ready for an amazing adventure in Hawai'i Volcanoes National Park?

# Welcome to Hawai'i Volcanoes National Park!

Hawai'i Volcanoes is located on the Big Island of Hawai'i. It was made a **national park** in 1916.

The park gets its name from two **active** volcanoes that are found there. Hot **lava** flows from the volcanoes!

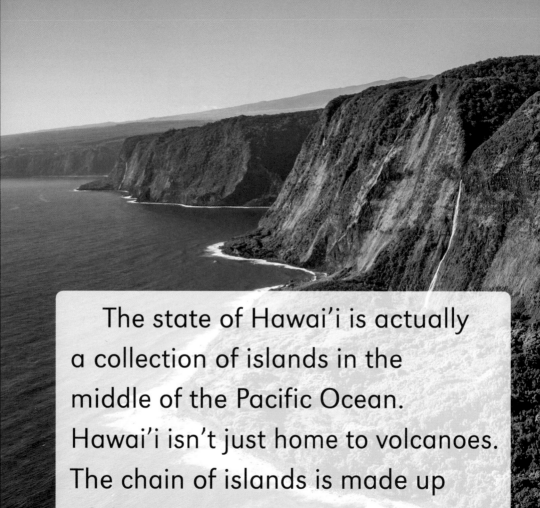

The state of Hawai'i is actually a collection of islands in the middle of the Pacific Ocean. Hawai'i isn't just home to volcanoes. The chain of islands is made up of them!

United States

Hawai'i

Hawai'i Volcanoes
National Park

Millions of years ago, lava burst from the seafloor. It piled up higher and higher and hardened into rock. Then more lava piled up and made more rock. This rock became the islands of Hawai'i.

Kilauea has been erupting since 1983. Not all of the eruptions are violent.

In 2018, explosive eruptions from Kilauea destroyed homes and forests. Much of the park had to close.

# Chapter 1

# Fiery Mountains

One of the park's volcanoes, Kilauea (kee-lah-**way**-ah), is one of the most active volcanoes in the world. Sometimes when Kilauea **erupts**, it blasts gases, rocks, ash, and lava into the sky. Lava is liquid rock. It is very hot and can cause a lot of destruction.

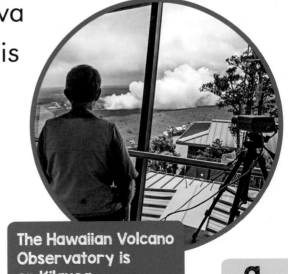

The Hawaiian Volcano Observatory is on Kilauea.

The last time Mauna Loa erupted was in 1984.

Mauna Loa is so tall that snow sometimes covers the top.

The other active volcano in the park is Mauna Loa (**maw**-nah **low**-ah). At 13,680 feet (4,179 meters) tall, Mauna Loa is the largest active

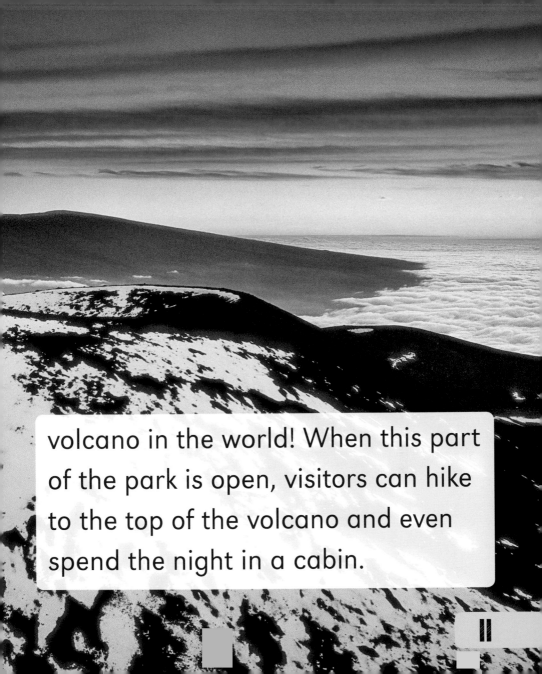

volcano in the world! When this part of the park is open, visitors can hike to the top of the volcano and even spend the night in a cabin.

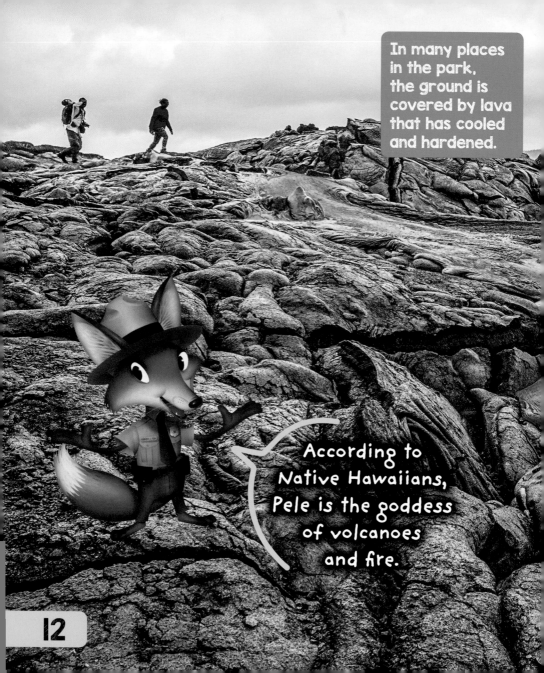

In many places in the park, the ground is covered by lava that has cooled and hardened.

According to Native Hawaiians, Pele is the goddess of volcanoes and fire.

# Chapter 2

# Lava Rocks!

Lava can be a'a (**ah**-ah) or pahoehoe (pah-**ho**-ee-ho-ee). A'a lava moves fast and has a spiky surface when it hardens. Pahoehoe lava moves slowly. Its surface has ripples when it hardens. Both types are found in the park.

a'a lava

pahoehoe lava

At the Kamokuna (**kah**-moh-koo-nah) lava delta, red-hot lava from Kilauea sometimes flows into the ocean. It can look like a waterfall of lava. As the scorching-hot lava touches the ocean water, it turns into rock. It also makes the ocean water boil and turn to steam.

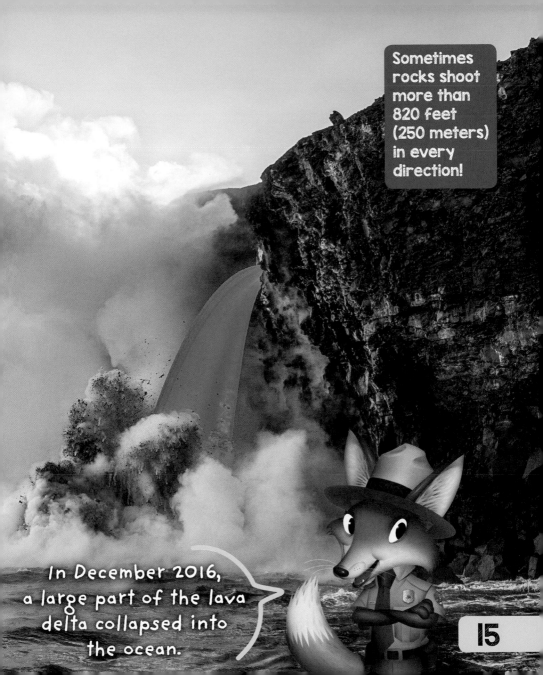

Sometimes rocks shoot more than 820 feet (250 meters) in every direction!

In December 2016, a large part of the lava delta collapsed into the ocean.

Sulfur in the steam makes the rocks at Sulphur Banks yellow.

Trees cannot grow near the steam vents at Sulphur Banks Trail. It is too hot for their roots!

# Chapter 3

# Sights and Smells

Some areas look like they're covered in smoke. That's caused by steam vents. The ground is so hot that water underneath turns to steam.

The steam that comes out of the ground at Sulphur Banks Trail smells like rotten eggs. That's because of a chemical in the water called sulfur.

The walk through the Thurston Lava Tube usually takes about 20 minutes.

The lava tube was discovered in 1913 by Lorrin Thurston. He helped create the park.

18

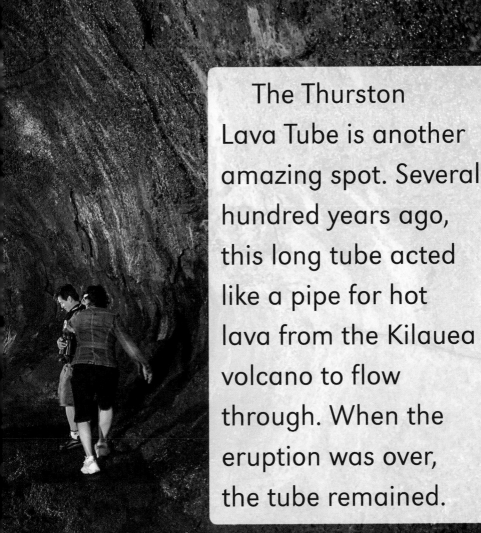

The Thurston Lava Tube is another amazing spot. Several hundred years ago, this long tube acted like a pipe for hot lava from the Kilauea volcano to flow through. When the eruption was over, the tube remained.

Visitors to the park can see sea turtles swimming in the surf.

# Chapter 4

# Wild Life

The park is home to many plants and animals. Some of them are found nowhere else in the United States. Nene (**nay**-nay) geese and songbirds fly through the skies. Crickets chirp as they hop over lava that just cooled. Hawksbill sea turtles come to the beaches to lay eggs.

The Hawaiian hoary bat sleeps upside down during the day.

Many of the park's plants like to grow in soil made from lava. Silverswords grow high up on the sides of the volcanoes. There are also wet rain forests filled with ferns and ohia lehua (oh-**hee**-ah lay-**hoo**-ah) trees. These trees with bright-red flowers are found only in the state of Hawai'i.

silversword plant

ohia lehua plant

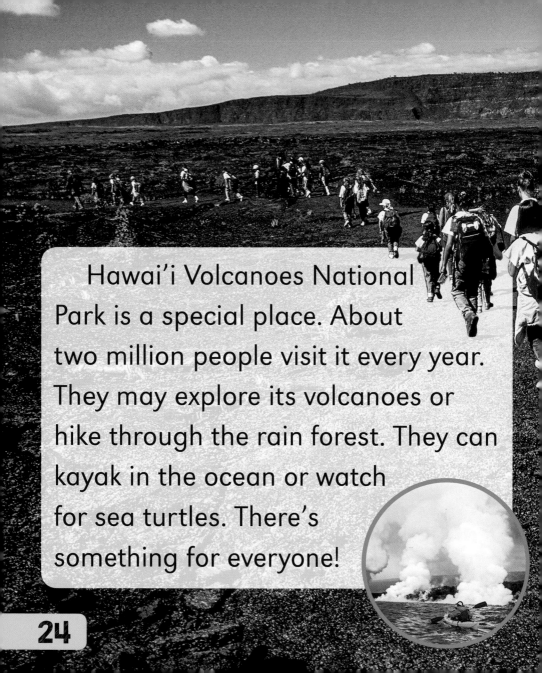

Hawai'i Volcanoes National Park is a special place. About two million people visit it every year. They may explore its volcanoes or hike through the rain forest. They can kayak in the ocean or watch for sea turtles. There's something for everyone!

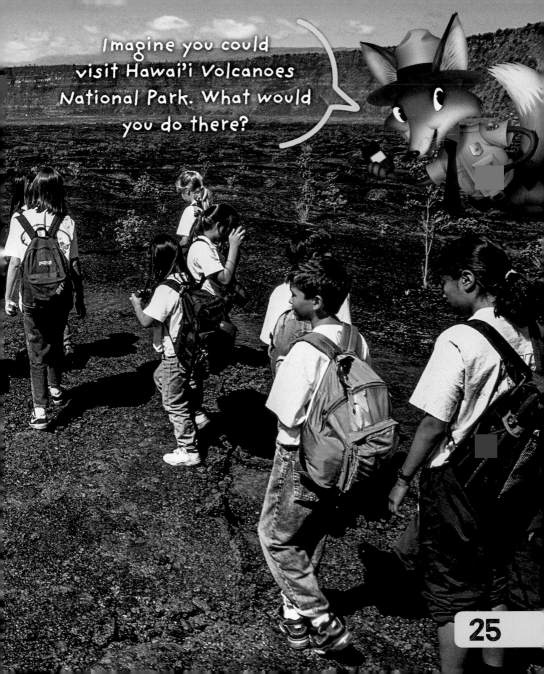

These are just some of the animals that make their home in Hawai'i Volcanoes National Park.

creeper tang

Hawaiian thrush

Hawaiian 'aholehole fish

common house gecko

Indian mongoose

spinner dolphin

## Wildlife by the Numbers

The park is home to about...

**62** types of birds     **14** types of mammals

The nene is the state bird of Hawai'i.

Hawaiian hawk

nene

wild pig

Hawaiian monk seal

mouflon sheep

**15** types of reptiles and amphibians

**4** native fish species

# Where Is Ranger Red Fox?

**Oh no! Ranger Red Fox has lost his way in the park. But you can help. Use the map and the clues below to find him.**

**1.** Ranger Red Fox started his adventure at the summit of Mauna Loa.

**2.** Then he headed east to walk through the Thurston Lava Tube and camp for the night.

**3.** When he woke up, he headed west to visit the Hawaiian Volcano Observatory.

**4.** Then he went southeast to see the lava flowing into the ocean.

Help! Can you find me?

# Hawai'i Volcanoes National Park

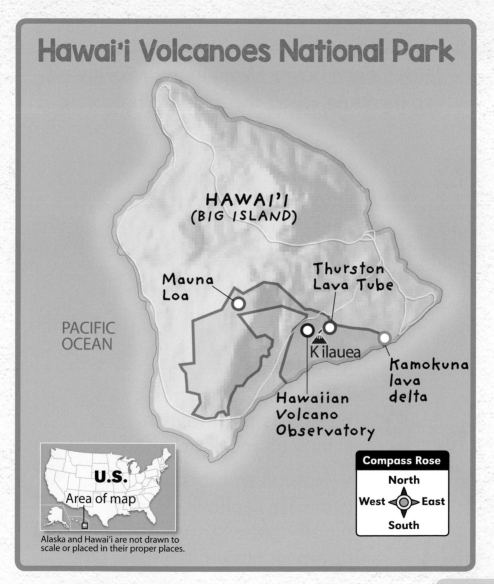

HAWAI'I
(BIG ISLAND)

Mauna
Loa

Thurston
Lava Tube

PACIFIC
OCEAN

Kilauea

Kamokuna
lava
delta

Hawaiian
Volcano
Observatory

U.S.
Area of map

Alaska and Hawai'i are not drawn to
scale or placed in their proper places.

Compass Rose
North
West ◉ East
South

# Wildflower Tracker

## Match each Hawai'i Volcanoes wildflower to its name. Read the clues to help you.

**A.**

**1. pikake (jasmine)**
Clue: Its beautiful smell gives away this white flower.

**2. bird-of-paradise**
Clue: Orange winglike petals give this flower its name.

**B.**

**C.**

**3. ohia lehua**
Clue: This flower has hundreds of petals as skinny as toothpicks.

**4. Hawaiian hibiscus**
Clue: This yellow bloom is the state flower of Hawai'i.

**D.**

30

# Glossary

**active** (**ak**-tiv): having erupted at least once in the past 10,000 years and may erupt again

**erupts** (**ih**-ruhpts): suddenly and violently throws out lava, hot ashes, and steam

**lava** (**lah**-vah): melted rock that flows or shoots from a volcano

**national park** (**nash**-uh-nuhl pahrk): area where the land and its animals are protected by the U.S. government

# Index

# Facts for Now

Visit this Scholastic Web site for more information
on Hawai'i Volcanoes National Park:
**www.factsfornow.scholastic.com**
Enter the keywords **Hawai'i Volcanoes**

# About the Author

**Karina Hamalainen** is an editor at Scholastic. She lives
in New York City, but she tries to escape the city and
explore the wilderness often.